Read All About Whales

WHALES AND PEOPLE

Jason Cooper

The Rourke Corporation, Inc.
Vero Beach, Florida 32964

PHOTO CREDITS
©Doug Perrine/INNERSPACE VISIONS: p.4,10, 22; ©Lynn M. Stone: p.7, 9,12,19; ©Marty Snyderman: p.13; ©Frank S. Balthis: p.20; ©Brandon Cole: p.15; ©Peter C. Howorth: p.6; ©Marilyn Kazmers/ INNERSPACE VISIONS: p.16; ©Gregory Ochocki: p.18; ©Thomas Kitchin: cover

Library of Congress Cataloging-in-Publication Data

Cooper, Jason, 1942-
    Whales and people / by Jason Cooper
        p. cm. — (Read all about whales)
    Includes index.
    Summary: Describes the changing relationship between whales and people, discussing how humans once hunted these air-breathing sea mammals and now work to save them from extinction.
    ISBN 0-86593-452-5
    1. Whales—Juvenile literature. 2. Human-animal relationships— Juvenile literature. [1. Whales. 2. Human-animal relationships 3. Rare animals. 4. Endangered species.]
    I. Title II. Series: Cooper, Jason, 1942- Read all about whales
QL737.C4C653 1996
599.5—dc20   96–19194
                                                                  CIP
                                                                   AC

Printed in the USA

TABLE OF CONTENTS

WHALES AND PEOPLE

Whales are among the most beloved animals in the world. It's not that they are furry and huggable. Whales have other charms. The great whales and their smaller cousins, the dolphins and porpoises, are intelligent and graceful. Often they are curious. They seem gentle, yet powerful.

Whales sometimes seem just a little like us. They are, after all, air-breathing **mammals** (MAM uhlz), as we are.

Most countries protect whales. Not long ago, though, whales were hunted by ships.

Bottle-nosed dolphins are perhaps the best known members of the whale family.

WHALERS

Many **species** (SPEE sheez), or kinds, of the biggest whales were nearly wiped out by whalers. Whalers are the people and ships that chased whales. Whalers roamed the seas from the Far North to the Far South, even among icebergs. Sailors spied whales when the animals rose to the ocean surface for a breath.

Whalers nearly wiped out the great blue whale, the largest animal on Earth.

A southern elephant seal lies in a garden of whale bones on South Georgia Island. Behind the seal is the old whaling village of Grytviken, now a ghost town.

Many countries killed whales from the 1600's into the 1900's. The United States became a whaling power in the mid 1800's.

WHALING WEAPONS

Whalers used metal **harpoons** (har POONZ) to kill whales. A harpoon is a heavy spear attached to a line on the ship.

In the late 1800's, whaling ships were made bigger and faster. Harpoons were armed with tips that exploded like little bombs. Whales became easier to chase and kill.

A ship at sea could catch, cut up, and store several whales.

A whaler's harpoon stands on the Petrel's deck. Once a whaler, it lies rusting at Grytviken in the Antarctic Ocean.

WHALE PRODUCTS

Whales were once more valuable dead than alive. That's why men in wooden ships once risked their lives to find them.

People used the oil in whales to fuel lamps and cooking stoves. People used whale meat for food, fertilizer, perfume, glue, medicine, and soap. Whalers began to search every corner of the oceans for whales.

The value of whale products very nearly caused the **extinction** (ex TINGK shun) of these animals.

A bottle of sperm whale oil from the old whaling town of New Bedford, Massachusetts, is displayed at Whaler's Village Museum in Maui, Hawaii.

THE END OF WHALING

Several species of whales just missed extinction, or disappearing altogether. By the 1900's, whalers had almost wiped out blue whales and some of the other big whales.

Grytviken's whale factory for Antarctic whalers closed in the 1960's. More than 110,000 whales were cut up here between 1904-1939.

A snorkeler swims with a huge right whale. The rights were brought close to extinction by whalers.

Meanwhile, people had begun to find substitutes for whale products. Oil pumped from the ground, for example, replaced the need for whale oil.

Still, a few whalers continued to prowl the seas. The last big whaling station in the Antarctic region did not close until the 1960's.

WHALES TODAY

America and most other countries are now trying to keep whales alive. They hope to rebuild the number of big whales to what they used to be. After all, no one really *needs* whale products any more. Japan and Norway, however, continue to kill several hundred minke whales each year. Iceland may begin a whale hunt.

People love to see whales. Boats take thousands of people to watch wild whales. Thousands more watch healthy whales at huge public **aquariums** (uh KWAR ee uhmz), zoos, and entertainment parks.

A humpback whale rises from the seas of Southeast Alaska to watch whale watchers. Humpbacks were nearly wiped out by the whaling industry.

WHALES IN DANGER

Most of the big whale species are still rare. Whales need many years of protection to rebuild their herds. A whale bears only one calf at a time.

The U.S. Fish and Wildlife Service lists eight whales and two river dolphin species as **endangered** (en DAYN jerd). These animals may still be in danger of disappearing.

Some whales are in much more danger than others. The California gray whales, for example, are doing well. They were recently removed from the Endangered Species List.

California gray whales are doing well. Whale watchers in Magdalena Bay, Mexico, admire a gray whale calf.

PROBLEMS FOR WHALES

Whales are protected almost everywhere. However, they still face danger. River dolphins face the real possibility of extinction. Many of the rivers in South America and Asia are filthy with pollution.

The rare Amazon river dolphin faces pollution and hunting in South America.

Biologists in Florida work to save a sick pygmy killer whale at Mote Marine Laboratory.

Another problem for certain whales is overfishing. When fishing boats take too many fish, fish-eating sea creatures cannot get enough to eat.

Fishing nets sometimes catch whales, dolphins, and porpoises. Oil spills at sea are also a danger for whales.

SAVING WHALES

America helps to save whales in many ways. U.S. law makes it illegal to kill whales and their cousins. It also forbids people from bringing whale products into the country.

Many people are helping to save whales by learning more about their habits. Their studies are often supported by the National Marine Fisheries Board.

Young people can help, too, by supporting groups that work to keep the oceans clean and to control fishing.

This young gray whale became tangled in a fishing boat's nets. Because it could not eat or swim properly, it died and washed ashore.